www.Pamelajdowning.com.

Throw Away The Excuses
And Succeed
Ignite Your Dreams And Goals

Dr. Pamela J. Smith-Downing

To all those trailblazers
who threw away their excuses
and
succeeded against all odds…

Contents

We are made for larger ends
than Earth can encompass.
Oh, let us be true to our exalted destiny.
Catherine Booth

Introduction

THROW AWAY THE excuses and succeed has been my mantra for so many years. Through various life tragedies, with the help of God in my life, I was able to triumph over all the tragedies in my life, and I refocused on the dreams and goals that were before me. I can recall looking at my biography, and the constant variable years after years was this phrase, "she is pursuing this or she is pursuing that." Well, I got fed up with the word "PURSUING" and decided to focus on the word "MANIFESTING."

As a result of transforming pursuing into manifesting as it relates to my dreams and goals, I accomplished a lot of dreams and goals in a short span of time. In Proverbs 13:19 (KJV), it states, "Desire fulfilled is sweet to the soul." [1] I am excited to encourage you, readers, to throw away all the excuses and succeed, regardless of your current situation, so that you can experience the sweetness of your desires. There are not too many excuses that a person can throw at me that I did not overcome and kept on manifesting right in the middle of all the obstacles.

In the late Dr. Miles Monroe book, "Understanding

Your Potential, Discovering, The Hidden You." [2] He states the following; "Though it may surprise you, the richest deposits on our planet lie just a few blocks from your house. They rest in your local cemetery or graveyard."

Yes, you read it correctly, he said the graveyards. People allowed other people to talk them right out of so many opportunities, leading them to bury those dreams and goals with them in the grave. Throw away the excuses and succeed should be a mantra for everyone because the only person that can stop you from succeeding in a specific area are the excuses you allow to take root in your life. Don't allow yourself nor anyone else to stop you from succeeding in your life. Let's get ready for a transformation in your life. GET READY TO THROW AWAY ALL THE EXCUSES AND START SUCCEEDING!

WATCH YOUR THOUGHTS
FOR THEY BECOME WORDS
WATCH YOUR WORDS
FOR THEY BECOME ACTIONS
WATCH YOUR ACTIONS
FOR THEY BECOME HABITS
WATCH YOUR HABITS
FOR THEY BECOME CHARACTER
WATCH YOUR CHARACTER
FOR IT BECOMES YOUR DESTINY
" Lao Tzo"

Watch Your Words

CHAPTER I:
Watch Your Words

MOST FOLKS HEARD the statement, "stick and stones may break your bones, but words will never hurt you." This is certainly not a true statement. In fact, we form words, and words can hurt or help us. The average conversation rate for English speakers in the United States is 150 wpm.[1] WOW! 150 wpm, can you imagine how many words we are speaking throughout the day? Now imagine how many words are actually words that can hurt us. Please dear reader, ponder on these questions below.

How many times throughout the day, did you tell yourself what you could not do because it was so overwhelming? How many times did you allow yourself to talk YOU out of a promotion? How many times throughout a day, did you allow yourself to agree with someone else who felt you could not go after that dream? How many times throughout the day did you say I am not worthy of pursuing that business? Single persons, how many times did you allow your words to say to yourself, I will never get married? Married persons, how many times did you say with your words, this marriage will never work? And finally, how many times did you speak out of your own mouth and ask, what's the use, it will never come to fruition for me? Watch those hurtful words that YOU are allowing to come out of your mouth.

You are speaking every minute, and yes, your words do carry weight. Your words can be hurtful or helpful, and it's up to you to make the transformation. I can recall working with a deaf person many years ago. For some reason, I was a little naive and thought that deaf persons were sweet all the time. Well, I got a rude awakening when that deaf co-worker was actually utilizing obscene sign languages to make her point. So even if you do not speak with a human tongue, watch your words while utilizing any type of communication tool. We are in the information age, and words are all around us.

People are utilizing all forms of social media to express their words. However, there so many hurtful words on social media. The question is, are we contributing to some of those hurtful words? Perhaps you posted a negative post about yourself, so why are you upset when people you do not know personally are commenting negatively about your post? People are posting with words like "they don't have the strength to accomplish a task," "they are having a bad day today," and many more negative words. Watch your words!

Again, it is imperative that you watch your words as you are transforming into a person of action with words. Stop saying "I CAN'T"! As long as you are proclaiming I CAN'T instead of I CAN, you will have exactly what you say. The words "I CAN'T" were actually curse words in our home. Our children were corrected numerous times when they said they could not do this or do that. However, we had to quickly remind them that they could do anything they put their minds to, and that included excelling in their academics, sports, piano lessons, martial arts, gymnastics, etc.

Why were we so adamant of ensuring that our children learned the principle of the power of words early on as children? Well, we wanted to take away all the excuses that they were trying to muster up about failing, and we were not going to accept their excuses. We knew they could excel in any area if they were willing to do the work to succeed. Therefore; we wanted to make sure all excuses in their minds were thrown away so it would not come out of their mouths. We were training our children to be successful in sending out positive words into the atmosphere and denouncing every negative word.

Now, as I begin to start saying what I wanted to see come to pass in my life in the various areas in my life, and you will read about some of those in this my book. I had to take every negative word into captivity and only release the positive words. I had to really practice what the Bible says about being quick to listen and slow to speak (James 1:19 KJV) [2] Although circumstances around me were not always pleasant, I had to decide if I was going to speak what I see or speak in faith what I wanted to manifest.

For example, instead of me saying, "I don't have the income for this specific project," I had to rephrase that statement with "I will have the money for that project." I recently wrote a book entitled "Read My Lips No More Debt". [3] In this book, I wrote about the importance of delayed gratification. I did not have to say, "I don't have the money," but adapt the principle of delayed gratification. I adjusted my words and priorities to line up with the fact that I may not have it now, but it is on the way. I refused to have my words speak negativity about that project. We want to utter words throughout the day that can help us, not hurt us. Watch your Words and throw away those negative words and succeed. Don't procrastinate, do it today.

List All Your Gift and Talents... Don't Be Shy

_____

_____

_____

_____

_____

_____

_____

_____

_____

_____

_____

_____

_____

_____

_____

_____

_____

_____

_____

Procrastination

CHAPTER 2:
Procrastination

PROCRASTINATION IS ONE of the major enemies on your path to success. Procrastination was once an enemy to me as well. I knew that I had various things that were birthed in me to accomplish but I kept putting those things off that were dear to me. However, I did not know how to balance helping others and yet still going after specific dreams and goals that were in me as well. I found myself doing for others and neglecting my dreams and goals. Once, I received the wisdom to balance all the demands on my life, I was now ready to throw away procrastination once and for all and move forward with working on dreams and goals almost daily. I now had the freedom to manifest in every area of my life the things God had planned for my life. No more procrastination excuses for me!

How many times have you told yourself I would complete this project or some other tasks? How many times did you give yourself a time limit to complete a certain assignment to only find yourself once again failing to complete the assignment? How many times did a year come in and go out with your same to do list untouched? Why are you sabotaging your own destiny with procrastination? Well, if you are going to succeed you must throw away one of the major excuses that too many people utilize and that is procrastination.

Webster defines procrastination as to put off intentionally and habitually (Meridian-Webster, n.d.).[1] Did you read that? You have a key role in procrastination you are putting your dreams and goals off and you are doing it intentionally and habitually.

You are getting too comfortable with making excusing why you did not complete your dreams and goals. If you are going to move forward you must conquer procrastination. You must start spending time on your dreams and goals while still celebrating others along the way. I am a huge cheerleader for other people; especially those who achieve milestones in their lives but I refuse to always celebrate others and not go after the dreams and goals that I want to accomplish as well.

In order for you to conquer procrastination, ask yourself these questions; what am I afraid of? Why am I always putting off my goals and dreams? Why do I make excuses about why I did not achieve my goals and dreams at the appointed time? Why do I not add time on my schedule throughout the week to achieve my goals and dreams? Reader, if you are honest with yourself like I was many years ago, you will find out that you can change your behavior and start moving forward with your dreams and goals.

You have everything you need to fulfill that dream or goal that seems impossible right now, however; you must end the procrastination cycle. You must realize that your dreams are important too. I lead a very demanding life; with many people depending on me daily but every day I manage to take time out for me. I manage my 24 hours to assist others but I don't forget about putting a meeting with myself on my calendar as well. I've heard testimonies from so many people of the things they were going to do; to only find them still not pursuing those dreams and goals but making excuses of why they could not accomplish it.

Procrastination is designed to keep you frustrated on every level. Have you ever experienced completing a task? Do you re-call the feeling you experienced when you completed that task? Perhaps it was a house project, a car project, or completed an on-line course whatever it was; think back to that feeling of accomplishment. How did it make you feel? I can tell you that I felt joy, all of my happy brain chemicals were working. I had accomplished one more task and I conquered procrastination regarding that specific project. You did as well, let's keep our happy brain chemicals working daily.

Refuse to let procrastination demand our days with frustrations and guilt. Don't let procrastination rob you of what you were destined to accomplish on this earth. Light a fire and get moving on those dreams and goals. Throw away procrastination once and forever and start succeeding.

Write Down Your Fears and Then Cross Them ALL Out

_____

_____

_____

_____

_____

_____

_____

_____

_____

_____

_____

_____

_____

_____

_____

_____

_____

_____

Throw Away Personal Excuses

CHAPTER 3:
Throw Away Personal Excuses

PERSONAL EXCUSES COME in all shapes and forms. Let's examine some of the major ones you may have heard of or experienced yourself. Some folks have made an excuse around their age. They feel that since they are no longer at a specific age, they can no longer fulfill their goals and dreams. As long as you are still breathing, that's enough reason for you to continue with your dreams and goals.

I love the famous Kentucky Fried Chicken Story. Colonel Sanders, at the age of 65, began Kentucky Fried Chicken, when most folks were only thinking about retiring. [1] You are never too old to go after your dreams and goals. If Colonel Sanders can become an entrepreneur at retirement age, what is your excuse? He became an entrepreneur at the age when most folks are looking forward to retiring.

Some folks even utilize their families as excuses for not achieving certain goals and dreams. I had heard folks make statements like, "when my kids get older, I will do this or do that." They end up having more excuses when they are grown and out of their homes. It is possible to achieve dreams and goals and have a family as well if you desire. You must throw away all the personal excuses and start on the path to your destiny.

Some folks have the excuses of being married, single, divorced, single parent, widow, widower, caregiver, etc. Well, you may be serving in some of these roles now, but don't let them become excuses for achieving your goals. There are many people who are serving in these roles, but they have accomplished goals and dreams while juggling the demands of their life. I am certainly one of those persons.

There are numerous support groups to assist you wherever you may be in life. Most religious organizations and various non-profits have awesome support groups to assist you in whatever role you are currently in today. Perhaps you are a single person raising children, there is support for you, seek it out. You can also partner up with other single parents and assist each other while acquiring your dreams and goals. You may be married and need a support group to assist you because you do not have that support group in your spouse, seek out a close friend but don't abort your dream. You may be divorced and don't know where to turn, there is support for you. Many divorcees have achieved numerous dreams and goals. Don't let personal excuses be an excuse for you to abort your destiny.

Years ago, there was a gentleman that I was encouraging to go after a specific dream and goal that he shared with me and his family. For years, he kept saying that he wanted to complete this specific assignment. Well, he started but never finished because he kept using his family as an excuse but even after his children had become adults, he still did not complete his assignment, and I often wondered how many people could have been encouraged as a result of him completing his assignment. He was the total opposite of his spouse because she was determined to go after her dreams and goals while balancing her family and career. As a result of his wife's successes, jealousy entered his heart and caused a lot of friction in their marriage.

When I was going back to college to finish up my first degree, my husband was on an overseas assignment. I was determined to get my associate degree while working on rotating shifts in the IT field. It was very challenging, but I relied on friends to watch our children. I disciplined myself to study, and I graduated with honors. I refused to use the fact that I was in a season of being a single parent while my husband was serving overseas to be an excuse why I could not go back to school and achieve my first degree.

I could have easily said that it's too hard, juggling the children back and forth, working rotating shifts, and being a leader in my local church. However, I took the challenge on and put in the work I needed to succeed, and succeed I did. What's your excuse? Don't let personal excuses stop you from achieving those goals and dreams. Also, you may not have the support of certain family members when you are going after your dreams and goals, and that's ok because others will be there for you. You must keep making progress, so you will obtain those goals. Remember whose dream and goals they are anyway.

Also, before I end this chapter, let me address this issue as well as it relates to personal excuses, PRIDE… Yes, PRIDE… Many persons have also embrace pride in their personal excuses. You will need to throw away your pride and realize that you will need someone to assist you with personal goals occasionally, but how can people assist if you are prideful. It's ok to tell a trusted friend or trusted relative that you need assistance. I am so thankful to the people who came and assisted me with my children while I was in school, but they would not have known I needed assistance if I had not reached out to them for assistance. Again lay aside pride, so you won't sabotage your own destiny.

This leads me into a testimonial from a real person. I assisted this person on her path to reaching her destiny. She was a single parent, and she was homeless at one point in her life. She complained about her situation, and she allowed pride to enter in as well. However, as a result of encouraging this person for years, she was able to realize that life is truly full of various seasons, and seasons will change. At the time of this writing, she is moving into her very own home, which was built from the ground up for her family. She worked hard and went back to school while throwing away her pride, and now she is on her way to achieving more goals in her life. She finally threw away all the excuses that life throw at her and persevered. Now she is in a position to help others as well.

I can recall sacrificing many hours of my personal

time and my finances to assist many single parents and married persons as they were on their way to fulfilling their destinies. I became babysitters to single parents and married parents while they went to work and school. I am still assisting others in various forms because I don't want anyone in my area of influence to leave this earth without fulfilling their God ordained destiny.

Whatever category you are in today, I admonish you to throw away the personal excuses and start achieving your goals and dreams. Be mindful of any pride that creeps in along with any personal excuses. Throw away those personal excuses and succeed.

List Your Personal Action Plans

_____

_____

_____

_____

_____

_____

_____

_____

_____

_____

_____

_____

_____

_____

_____

_____

_____

_____

Throw Away Financial Excuses

CHAPTER 4:
Throw Away Financial Excuses

THERE ARE MANY people who are utilizing money excuses. They use money as an excuse as to why they cannot achieve their dreams and goals. This can't be further from the truth. In my book *Read My Lips No More Debt,* [1] I stated statistics on how much Americans are spending. If you take a good look at your spending habits, you will find out how much money you can actually put towards your financial goals to succeed with your dreams and goals.

There are many financial avenues that can help you achieve your dreams and goals. As long as you have finance labeled as an excuse, it will be an excuse. You must seek out opportunities to assist you in achieving your goals. For example, when I was going back to school, I sought out scholarships. I applied for many scholarships since I was an honor student. I was awarded scholarships to assist me on my educational path. I was not going to allow financial excuses to stop me from obtaining my degrees. I also sacrificed and paid cash for my college expenses as well.

There will be a financial cost for some dreams and goals. The question is, will you make it an excuse, or will you seek out ways to make your dreams become a reality, regardless of the cost? It may require you taking on a second job, working overtime, etc. How bad do you want to achieve your dreams and goals? Don't let finances become an excuse, you can achieve those dreams and goals with passion and determination. You are gifted, and you can utilize the gifts and talents you possess already to obtain financing.

In the Bible, there is a very important passage about finances concerning the individual. In Deuteronomy 8:18, it states, "But thou shalt remember the Lord thy God: for it is He that giveth the power to get wealth" [1]. I was sharing with one of my mentees, the possibility of her owning her own food truck one day. She is very gifted in the area of southern cooking, and she can make extra income as a side gig to bring in extra finances to support her dreams and goals.

She did not have to look anywhere because her gifts and talents provided extra income for her. What about you? What gifts and talents are you possessing to bring in extra finances? Do you like pets? Seek out becoming a pet sitter. Can you work on computers? Are you a social media guru? Can you clean houses? Can you proofread documents? Can you sing? Can you cut lawns? The areas of possibilities are endless regarding acquiring additional income.

I met a nurse in 2020, and he shared with me that he was accepted to medical school. I was so excited for him. However, he went on to give me a whole litany of excuses why he could not go to medical school. I told him that he must take each accomplishment as a steppingstone to the next path along the way. I explained to him, "if you received the acceptance to medical school, you can seek out avenues that will assist you financially along the way." Again, how many people have thrown away their dreams and goals because of financial obstacles. Finance is just another obstacle that you will have to throw away on your path to success. Don't buy into this excuse. Once again research ways to finance your dreams and goals. Throw away the finance excuses and succeed.

List Your Financial Action Plans

_____

_____

_____

_____

_____

_____

_____

_____

_____

_____

_____

_____

_____

_____

_____

_____

_____

_____

Throw Away Higher
Learning Excuses

CHAPTER 5:
Throw Away Higher Learning Excuses

I HEARD SO MANY people make the following statement, "I wish I could go back to school, but I can't." This could not be further from the truth. As long as you continue to say you can't, then you will not achieve your higher learning success. Again, watch your words. The achievement of walking across that stage is a sense of accomplishment that no one can take from you, but you must throw away the excuses of why you cannot achieve success in higher learning.

At one point, I was in the following roles at the same time, married, raising children, care giver to my mother, full time employment, personal tragedies, CEO of No Child Left Alone (non-profit), CEO of PJD Enterprises, LLC, Co-founder of a local church, and college student, but I was determined to get my Doctoral degree, and I graduated Summa Cum Laude. I share this personal testimony to encourage you to throw away all your higher education excuses and keep moving toward your dreams and goals.

Now you may be thinking, how can anyone possibly make that outstanding accomplishment and graduate as Summa Cum Laude with all the demands on their life? Well, when you are determined to achieve a specific goal, nothing and no one can stop you. I had to remain focus and see myself going across that platform to receive my doctoral degree. I was not about to let any excuse that I could have easily entertain stop and hinder me on my path of achieving my Doctoral degree.

I started planning my Doctoral gala before I received my Doctoral, and that also gave me momentum to complete my Doctoral on time with no delays. What a Gala it was, I was able to contract my favorite Gospel artist Helen Baylor and had the pleasure of singing with her on stage. Now, I am not a singer, but I was making a joyful noise that night. It was simply awesome to be surrounded by family and friends as we celebrated my accomplishments and as I gave Glory to God for sustaining me along the way. Please enjoy the pictures of the gala in the photo gallery.

Years ago, I gave one of my mentees a reading assignment, and she told me that she don't like to read, but she wanted to achieve a degree. I quickly asked her to never make that statement again. Reading is a part of learning, and you must get over the fear of higher education and exposing yourself to different topics that you are not accustomed to in life.

The first president of America, George Washington, did not have a formal education, however, he taught himself throughout his life because he read thousands of books on various topics. I am an avid reader, and I read about 2 ½ books a month on various topics. I love autobiographies and life lesson books because those folks have figured out a lot of things that I am seeking to learn, and they put them in books for me and others to dig out. Reader, whatever your desire regarding higher learning, go after them. Are you looking to get your Associate's, Bachelor's, Master's Degree, or Doctoral? Whatever level you are looking to achieve, go after it. Like I stated before, there are so many opportunities you can take advantage of, regarding your education.

The first step is to decide when you will start going back to school, not rehearsing the number of excuses why you can't. Go ahead and start doing your research on the physical school or online school you would like to start attending immediately. Again, seek out scholarships and whenever possible, start an education fund that is solely utilized for your education. You have conquered procrastination, and now you can throw away the excuses regarding higher education.

One of my daughter's friends heard about me achieving my 2nd Bachelor's degree in 2016 after achieving my Doctoral degree in 2014. He asked my daughter the following question "When is your mom going to stop going to school?" My answer was that "learning is a lifetime achievement." I will never stop learning and never stop pursuing and achieving learning opportunities.

It's never too late to go back to achieve any degree or any specialized training. I am so glad that Ms. Nola Ochs did not convince herself that at the age of 95, she was too old to get a college degree. [1] She is the oldest person to achieve this accomplishment at the time of this writing. Wow! At the age of 95, what an inspiration to all who are seeking higher education.

Can you imagine the many excuses Ms. Ochs could have easily given herself, but she was determined to get her college degree despite her age. Again, what an inspiration to all who have a love for higher education!? Go after your higher educational goals by throwing away all your excuses and succeed.

List Your Higher Educational Action Plans

_____

_____

_____

_____

_____

_____

_____

_____

_____

_____

_____

_____

_____

_____

_____

_____

_____

_____

_____

_____

Throw Away Entrepreneur Excuses

CHAPTER 6:
Throw Away
Entrepreneur Excuses

FOR THOSE WHO are considering entrepreneurship, let's take a look at the following business statistics. According to data from the Census Bureau's Annual Survey of Entrepreneurs, there were 5.6 million employer firms in the United States in 2016. Firms with fewer than 500 workers accounted for 99.7 percent of those businesses. Firms with fewer than 100 workers accounted for 98.2 percent. Firms with fewer than 20 workers made up 89.0 percent. There were 24.8 million in 2016 (latest data) – then the share of U.S. businesses with less than 20 workers increases to 98.0 percent [1].

Bottom line, small businesses make up 96% of the jobs in America. Innovation and passion are the common thread for all business owners. Entrepreneurs throw away excuses and solve problems for specific customers. What is the problem that you want to solve for customers? How about a cause you want to bring awareness to as a non-profit? Do you want to own your own restaurant? A food truck for area workers? Or how about a specific product that you invented, or a specific expertise that you can offer to customers? The entrepreneurship opportunities are endless.

COVID-19 exposed just how important our small businesses are to Americans. Many of us could not wait to get our favorite food take-outs. We were bombarding our personal care services from specific areas of expertise, when it was safe to return to their physical locations. We rallied around our business owners and celebrated their return to serve us all.

However, instantly there were new entrepreneurs in the midst of COVID-19. Entrepreneurs, who were suddenly making masks with various designs and sparkly gems. Some entrepreneurs started outside services to take care of children, and the creativity juices started to flow all across the USA. As a result, many new entrepreneurs were birthed all around the world in 2020 due to COVID-19.

What excuses do you have, when people who were innovative and passionate went after their dreams and goals right in the middle of a pandemic? What business idea has been buried for years inside of you? Well, now it's time to resurrect that idea. Throw away the excuses and start today on your road to becoming an entrepreneur. You have what it takes to become an entrepreneur. When I started my first business, I had the same thoughts that many of you may experience, and that is failure.

However, I had to push through those thoughts

and launch out anyway. Don't be concerned with the naysayers; just keep moving forward with your dreams of launching your own business. How many people are depending on you?

Also, remember failure is not bad. I applaud everyone who had the passion to reach out and achieve that business idea, even if it did not turn out as planned. However, if you never take the risk, you will never know what areas you need to improve on with that business plan or idea. What services can you offer to assist families and your communities? Can you imagine if the many places we love to shop, eat, receive personal services did not exist because the person was fearful of starting the business? Well, I'm glad my favorite car service businesses, dry cleaners, hair salons, restaurants, shopping arenas were established. I am grateful for all those businesses, and I am thankful that they did not abort their passion for meeting a need in our community.

Move forward with your business ideas and create a need that will keep customers coming due to your excellent customer services. Go ahead and throw away the excuses and start making your business plans for your next business adventure and join the millions of entrepreneurs who are serving customers all over the world. Every entrepreneur did not get all areas right during their first attempt at entrepreneurship, but they kept on dreaming. Don't let that dream die with you in the graveyard!

List Your Business Action Plans

_____

_____

_____

_____

_____

_____

_____

_____

_____

_____

_____

_____

_____

_____

_____

_____

_____

_____

_____

Throw Away Health Excuses

CHAPTER 7:
Throw Away Health Excuses

HOW MANY TIMES have you made or heard those famous New Year's resolutions concerning our weight programs? We promised to exercise more, we promised to eat our vegetables more, we promised to drink more water, and the list goes on and on… Well, we all know what to do, but we are not committed and consistent to doing what we need to do when it comes to our health. Now, I must say that I was GUILTY too… I had a great regiment years ago that I was committed to, I had my hour walk a day and eating healthy, but it only lasted about 3 months. Why was that? I was not committed. I made excuses, especially when I saw my husband eating what he wanted to eat, and I was eating my veggies and drinking my water. I know it sounds funny, huh?

However, all I did was allow my husband to be my excuse for not being committed to my exercise plan. You see once again, whose dreams, and goals are they anyway? That's right! It's your goal, so you must stay committed to your health goals. Now let's examine these startling health statistics regarding obesity in America.

- Non-Hispanic blacks (49.6%) had the highest age-adjusted prevalence of obesity
- Hispanics (44.8%) had the second age-adjusted prevalence of obesity
- Non-Hispanic whites (42.2%) had the third age-adjusted prevalence of obesity
- Non-Hispanic Asians (17.4%) had the forth age-adjusted prevalence of obesity
- The prevalence of obesity was 40.0% among young adults aged 20 to 39 years
- The prevalence of obesity was 44.8% among middle-aged adults aged 40 to 59 years
- The prevalence of obesity was 42.8% among adults aged 60 and older. [1]

WOW! We must do a better job of throwing away the excuses regarding our health and stay committed to eating healthy and exercising daily. We all know what to do; we just have to do it. The COVID-19 pandemic around the world exposed that those with underlined health conditions were the most vulnerable to the disease as well. When we are healthy, we can certainly accomplish a lot of things in our lives because we have the energy to produce on all levels in our lives.

Begin to start a regimen that fits you, with so many exercise plans and eating styles for you to choose from, you must decide what is best for you. The bottom line is that you start somewhere. Don't be overwhelmed with the choices, just start somewhere. For example, you can decide today that I am going to consume more water than any other beverage I drink today. You can also decide that I am going to limit my sugar intake daily and perhaps make several days during the week a no sugar day. Again, these are just suggestions that you can begin to see just how easy it can be to start eating healthy, but again, it all starts with you. There is something to the statement if you want to break a habit, commit to stop doing a specific habit for 21 days.

Every year, our local church engages in a 40 day fast during Lent season. During the fast, we commit as a church to eat healthy and drink healthy. We refrain from all sugar, fried foods, breads, etc. We eat vegetables, baked chicken, or fish with scales. We drink water and 100% juice with no sugar for 40 days. The results from some who are committed to the fast every year is astounding. Of course, your body will go through withdrawals from being used to all the sugar, fatty foods, etc. However, once the withdrawal phase is over, normally three days, you are on your way to a healthy lifestyle for the next 40 days. Some have committed to this lifestyle after the fast.

I can recall years ago while on one of our church's annual 40 days fast, I was not eating any more of my beloved Strawberry Twizzlers. When the fast ended, the next week, I wanted a couple of my Twizzlers. I proceeded to enjoy my favorite candy, and to my surprise, I was not enjoying my Twizzlers. It tasted awful to my taste buds, and my 10-year love affair with Twizzlers ended. I started a habit of not eating those Twizzlers for 40 days, and it broke the cycle of me craving Twizzlers for that day on. I must admit I did try tasting one a month later just to test the waters, and once again, the taste was not there like before. Again, the important thing is that you begin somewhere as it relates to eating healthy.

Exercising does not have to be costly, again during the COVID-19, millions of folks did not have access to their gym facilities but made alternative methods of exercising. People included me, started walking in our neighborhoods. I also utilized my stairs to this day to walk up and down to keep my body healthy. You can find very exciting new avenues to exercise your body. If you are watching television, get up and move during the commercials.

In a chair or in bed, you can also exercise your legs and arms, as you can see, there are numerous ways to keep your body active. Remember, the ball is in your park, do you want to hang on to excuses, or do you want to get results as it pertains to maintaining a consistently healthy lifestyle. There were two comments when people saw friends and family members after some of the COVID-19 restrictions were lifted, WOW look at that COVID-19 weight loss or WOW! Look at that COVID-19 weight gain.

Again, when you are healthy you are able to produce more and more. Let your testimony be one of not becoming a junk food addict or coach potato, but you threw away all the exercise excuses. You throw away the excuses as it related to your health and took ownership of having a consistent healthy lifestyle, so you can go after those dreams and goals without delays.

Also, before I end this chapter, I want to commend all who are faced with very serious illnesses, but they are yet going forth with their dreams and goals. You all are indeed an inspiration to us all. I am often moved when I take the book The Last Lecture by Randy Pausch and Jeffery Zaslow[2] off of my bookshelf and read it again. If you have not read the book, please do so, it recounts the life of Randy Pausch.

He begins the book by stating that he only has about a few months to live, and at the time, he was raising three young boys. He died a few months after the book was published with pancreatic cancer at the age of 47. What an inspiring testimony of someone with so much passion to leave a legacy for his children, that despise his health issues he threw away all the excuses. He could have easily thrown every excuse about his health to the world, and we would have understood, but instead, he wanted to succeed with leaving his life story for his family and all to remember. SUCCEED he did!

Write Down Your Health and Exercise Plans

_____

_____

_____

_____

_____

_____

_____

_____

_____

_____

_____

_____

_____

_____

_____

_____

_____

_____

Throw Away Travel Excuses

CHAPTER 8:
Throw Away Travel Excuses

COVID-19 HAS CURTAILED a lot of travelling outside of America. My youngest brother Antoine decided to throw away the travel excuse, and since he was not able to work on his primary job due to COVID-19. He decided to take a cross country drive from Las Vegas to CT; CT to VA, and lastly from VA to Las Vegas. He mapped out famous barbecue take-out restaurants and visited the Dallas Cowboys Stadium (I had to mention his famous team). He refused to have an excuse why he was not able to travel, so he threw away the excuses and gave himself, his son Tyler and his two nephews Jonas and Jaeden memories that will last the rest of their lives in the middle of COVID-19.

What's your excuse? Why are you saying when I retire, I will go here and go there? Throw away the excuses and travel. I often tell people that I am living my life like a retiree. I am travelling to the various countries and states within the United States because I have planned and mapped out timeframes and costs throughout the year.

In 2020, I had an aggressive travel plan. In March of 2020, my husband and I were scheduled to be on the Dave Ramsey Debt Free cruise for my birthday travelling to Half Moon Cay, Turks & Caicos, St. Thomas and San Juan. In May of 2020, my daughter Joi and I were scheduled to be in Israel and Italy, and in October of 2020, I was scheduled to be in China and Tibet. Well, as we all know, the COVID-19 pandemic cancelled all trips in 2020. However, I can't wait to start travelling again to exciting countries. I refuse to live a life of fear and not enjoy the things that I am passionate about in this life, especially travelling to exciting and historic countries.

Sometimes you have to be willing to travel alone, and not make any excuses. Like I stated in a previous chapter about Israel, I went to Israel not knowing anyone on the trip but left with new friends and connections around the world. When the travel bands are lifted, throw away the excuses of why you are not able to travel. I can recall in 2018, my cousin Kimberly and I went to the Grand Canyon, and we met a person on the trip who was travelling by herself, she stated that none of her friends were able to come, but she decided to come anyway, she spent her entire trip with us taking pictures and having a blast. Don't let yourself or others talk you out of travelling.

At the time of this writing, I have travelled to 27 states in America; my goal is to visit all 50 states. I also travelled so far to 17 countries my goal is to visit at least 2 new countries every year. Enjoy the pictures from the photo gallery of some of my travel adventures around the world in the photo gallery section. Throw away the travel excuses and succeed; there is a huge world just waiting for you to enjoy and make lasting memories of a lifetime to share with others.

Write Down Your Desired Travel Locations

_____

_____

_____

_____

_____

_____

_____

_____

_____

_____

_____

_____

_____

_____

_____

_____

_____

_____

Throw Away Dreams and Goals Excuses

CHAPTER 9:
Throw Away Dreams and Goals Excuses

R EADER, THIS IS my most exciting chapter in this entire book. I want you to get inspired as you take a special journey with me. I want to share some of my past dreams and goals that have come to pass over a 30-year span at the time of this writing. My very first experience of having BIG dreams was when I was around the age of thirteen, sitting on the stairs on our front porch steps in New Haven, CT. I was glancing through a magazine, and the Eiffel tower in Paris, France, caught my attention. It caught my attention so strongly that something inside of me resonated to the point that I saw myself visiting the Eiffel Tower one day. Now, how would an African American person from a divorced single person home with six children visit the Eiffel tower in Paris, France? Well, you see, when the dream is igniting inside of you, the fire is lit, and the flames will begin to emerge from all over.

It wasn't until eight years later, at the age of 22, when I was in Paris, France visiting the Eiffel Tower that the dream I had as a little girl on the front steps was visited once again. As I visited the Eiffel Tower, my mind immediately went back to that teenage girl on the front steps that had a dream, and that teenage girl never stopped dreaming and setting goals. Not only was I able to visit Paris, France, but I was blessed in that same year to also visit Madrid and Barcelona, Spain, to include and many other cities throughout Europe. I was especially excited to visit and tour the oldest city in Germany, which is Trier.

Those who know me personally know that I never back off of a challenge as it relates to achieving dreams and goals that I desire to accomplish during a specific period of time. I love seeing the manifestation of what faith can produce for those who are willing to operate in faith and watch their dreams and goals come true. Those who do not achieve certain dreams and goals are masters at throwing excuses on why they cannot achieve those goals and dreams.

Some folks love blaming others, circumstances, and even themselves on why they can't accomplish certain dreams and goals. No one should give a person control of their destiny, you have the power within you to accomplish the desires you would like to accomplish. My desires and goals may not be what my spouse, relatives, or friends desires because it's mine. So be very careful that you don't abort dreams and goals that you want to accomplish because of naysayers or well-meaning family members.

I can recall that one of my dreams was to go to Israel in 2012, and I was planning my trip, and certain family members and friends were trying to talk me out of going to Israel because of what they were seeing on the news pertaining to some of the mounting unrest in Israel. I actually travelled to Israel with the Trinity Broadcasting Network (TBN) tour group. Family and friends were also concern that I was not going with someone I knew, but I was determined to go.

However, I was not naive to news reports, but again, I was determined to go to Israel. I went as far as to tell them because of my Christian faith, if I die in Israel, what a beautiful place to die. I had to put away all the fears that well-intended people wanted to throw my way and operate in faith.

Reader, my visit to Israel was the best trip I ever had in my life. I gain a new friend who was my roommate, and we laughed and made new memories in our lives. We were safe, and TBN accomplished an amazing Israel tour.

I share this story because you may have dreams and goals that may take you to other countries, or perhaps starting a new business or going back to school. Whatever it is, don't let anyone put fear on you that will allow you to abandon your faith. Including You! I have mentioned faith several times but let me give you a personal definition of faith. Faith is standing firm on dreams and goals and doing your part by working it out; until that dream and goal manifest.

For example, I told the family the dates I was going to Israel, I saw myself in Israel, visiting all the major historic sites, visiting the Dead Sea, being baptized in the Jordan River, and so many other events. I saw myself already there, so the only thing left was the funds to pay for the entire trip. I had to do my part, make deposits for the trip, and of course, be at the airport at the appointed time to make my airline connections, etc.

It's the same thing when it comes to any dreams and goals; see yourself doing it or achieving it and start doing your part to make it a reality. You will be amazed at how others will get on board with your vision and dreams to assist you as well, all because you released your faith in the atmosphere for your dreams and goals.

I also wanted to go to the Motherland, and I was able to accomplish that dream in 2013 when I had the opportunity to visit Kenya, Africa. What another life experience to meet beautiful people from Mombasa and Nairobi? I also had the pleasure of meeting beautiful people from the Mombazi Tribe and serve so many who were in need in Mombasa, Kenya. However, I was able to experience the Indian Ocean and enjoyed the Voyager Beach Resort, which is a beautiful resort in Kenya, Africa, and of course, enjoyed the wonderful unique shopping experience in Africa. You will read about my many other travel adventures around the world later on in this book.

As you read, when it came to my educational goals, I was determined to obtain my Doctoral Degree, and it took years and years to accomplish. I had several high demands on my life, but it did not stop me from achieving my educational goals and inspire others to throw away excuses and keep moving towards their education goals. Scholarships and employment opportunities were also there to assist with that goal. However, I already saw myself walking across the stage receiving degrees years before I obtained it, and I also wrote down action plans as well to keep the vision before me as well.

Well, that same type of intensity is present in every area of my life. I love seeing what my faith can manifest in any arena. I want to lay the foundation for you in this chapter that is basically the foundation that will help you achieve anything you want to in this life. Now, you may say, why didn't I put this chapter in the beginning of the book? Well, I wanted you to write down all your action plans because you are actually writing down your vision for those areas in your life.

Remember the statement that I made earlier that your dreams and goals are yours. Well, for years, my family had a faithful routine, and that was watching The Wheel of Fortune. We would celebrate with the contestants as if we won those prizes. One of my desires was to go to a Wheel of Fortune tryout. Well, years ago, the producers of Wheel of Fortune were conducting tryouts in the D.C. area, and I was fortunate with one of my nieces Kendra to go there for a tryout. I was so excited. I was determined to take advantage of this opportunity. Although I was not selected to go on stage, my niece Kendra was selected, I had the opportunity to be among contestants and take pictures. Enjoy the photos in the photo gallery of my Wheel of Fortune set adventure, as well as major hi-lights, VIPs, and fun activities.

The fire was ignited in my life at age thirteen to DREAM BIG, and I have not stopped dreaming and MANIFESTING. Throw away your EXCUSES!

Write Down Your Dreams and Goals

.

_____

_____

_____

_____

_____

_____

_____

_____

_____

_____

_____

_____

_____

_____

_____

_____

_____

_____

_____

_____

Succeed

CHAPTER 10:
Succeed

I SHARE THIS TESTIMONY with full permission from the person who so graciously shared it with me on December 3, 2020. I met John when my mother was battling acute pneumonia in Bon Secours Mercy Medical Center, located in Petersburg, VA. John was one of the Registered Nurses serving my mother. John's story was so uplifting that I had to ensure it was added to this publication.

John was a veteran with a family. However, the Army was downsizing in the late '80s and did not offer him an opportunity to re-enlist. As a result of him not being able to re-enlist and the mounting bills, his family eventually lost their home. Not soon after, his wife divorced him, and he had little contact with his children.

He lived in his car for a few months, but soon his car was reposed as well. John, a Veteran found himself living on the streets. "Although flawless counts are impossible to come by – the transient nature of homeless populations presents a major difficulty – the

U.S. Department of Housing, and Urban Development (HUD) estimates that 40,056 veterans are homeless on any given night".[1] John could not believe how his life had turned out and he thought about suicide frequently.

One of John's Army buddies found John and offered John a place to stay. John was grateful for the opportunity to get off the streets, but he did not want to be a loafer for long. One day, when John's friend left for work, John decided that he would kill himself. He took his friend's revolver and placed it to his head, but before he pulled the trigger, he said a prayer, "God, if you are real, please give me a sign that there is more to my life than what I am experiencing now." At that moment, John's friend's dog came out of nowhere and hit the remote control of the television, and the commercial was showing an ad from ECPI advertising to apply for the Registered Nursing position in Richmond, VA. John immediately put the gun down and searched out the qualifications for the Registered Nursing ECPI training.

John had no vehicle or money, but when he went online, the location for the training was only 1.5 miles from his friend's place. John walked to the location on that Friday and took the test. The head supervisor came out and said, John, you passed the test and all qualifications. John then asked, "What is the next step?" The supervisor replied report on Monday for training for the Registered Nurse program. The military will pay for your education, and you will receive a stipend every month while you are in training. John could not believe what he heard. As a result of saying a quick prayer and doing his part to investigate ECPI, his life was turned around in hours.

John met his 2nd wife on the first day of RN training (they sat right next to each other). They now have a daughter together, and he has re-united with all his children. John almost threw away his life, but he decided to give it one more try. I am so grateful that he did not end his life. John was one of the best caring and knowledgeable nurses my mother had serving her while she was in the hospital.

Thank you John, for throwing away the excuses of being let go from the Military, divorced, losing your children, jobless, homeless, but although you were at your lowest point, you SUCCEEDED. You went forth into a new career with passion and zeal and such a love for your patients. May you continue to spread your love and passion to every co-worker and every patient.

WOW! What a moving story! Now that all your excuses are thrown away, the rest is up to you. Yes, YOU…. Just like John, You are the main player in your life. God has gifted you with those gifts and talents, and now it's time for you to MANIFEST. John manifested into a caring RN from the ashes of Despair. It's amazing when you start throwing away excuses, people will be assigned to assist you along the way.

What did that supervisor see in John that made her determined to get him in the RN program as soon as possible? People will be there to assist with their words of encouragement, their finances, and their wisdom.

Are you going to be the first author in your family, the first business person, the first college graduate, the first world travel, the first artist? The first RN? The list can go on and on about what YOU can become now that the excuses are all thrown away.

Again it's up to YOU. Remember, procrastination and negative people are your enemies. Procrastination will always tell you that you don't have time to succeed. You are too tired, you can do it next week, and next week ends up being years. Your negative friends or family members will always have an opinion about your success, but what have they achieved in that specific area you are trying to achieve? How will you know you can achieve a certain milestone, if you don't first make attempts to achieve those goals? Yes, I said attempts, you can't throw in the towel just because you failed on the first attempt.

I truly admire President Abraham Lincoln's, the 16th President of the United States life accounts. [2] He failed in so many elections before he actually became the 16th President and he helped shaped the United States of America into the best nation on earth. What if President Lincoln decided to throw in the towel when he lost his first state legislature race in 1832? Well, for sure, there would be no Emancipation Proclamation on January 1, 1863, that abolished slavery. Since his first rejection in politics, it took thirty-one years for Lincoln to overcome more political obstacles but eventually fulfilled his greatest destiny in history, abolishing slavery. President Lincoln threw away many excuses to include childhood tragedies, family loss, and business loss, to achieve his many successes.

Be careful whose opinion you allow to determine your success. Sometimes, it can be a mentor who may be a little jealous of you and tell you that that dream or goal will not work. However, you must remind yourself that it's your dream.

I can recall when I decided to enlist in the U.S. Army years ago, one of my mentors told me you are too girly for the military, you won't make it in the military. Well, those words really hurt, but I did not let her opinion stop me from going into the military. I would have never met my husband and all the wonderful people I met along the way as I served our country. Later on, I found out that the reason she made those comments was because she did not want to see me go since I was her best assistant.

Your success will not come without struggles, but you must keep your goals ahead of you. You may experience extreme family issues, tragedies, betrayals, job issues, health issues, I did, but you must keep moving forward on your pathway to your success.

Remember also that you are not selfish when it comes to going after your dreams and goals. These are your dreams and goals, and don't you let ANYONE talk you out of them. I can recall being questioned when I took my first trip to Israel in 2012. I received comments like, "You are going there by yourself?" "It's dangerous over there." If I had let those well-meaning people's comments stop me from going to Israel, I would have missed out on one of the most spiritual encounters in my life, especially getting baptized and baptizing others in the Jordan river.

Reader, you must succeed for yourself and for others. So many people are in awe of a lot of my accomplishments, but I accomplished all that I have done so far with the help of God and with a deep determination to let no one stop me. We all have 24 hrs in a day, the difference between those who are just surviving and those who are focused on their dreams and goals is that those who are focused takes advantage of every hour and can account for those hours. Those who are not focused will always have this comment "I don't know where the day went."

I have never been a big fan of watching TV the majority of my time, or spending too much time on social media. My life is filled with projects, so my time is very much guarded on being productive. Even on vacations, I am being productive, I may read a great book while relaxing or meditating on my next book or event. Dreams and goals are always on my mind because there is so much to accomplish, and so little time to do it.

Your family and friends are a part of your dreams and goals because they are always benefiting from your manifestation in one way or another. SUCCEED, and don't you be ashamed of your good success. Enjoy this quote from the Bible Proverbs 3:4 (ESV) [3] "So you will find favor and good success in the sight of God and man." Go after good success, and God will do the rest.

Reader, in the words of Zig Ziglar,
"I won't just see you at the top,
I will see you over the top." [4]
THROW AWAY THE EXCUSES
AND SUCCEED!

Thank You!

To my Lord and Savior Jesus Christ for walking with me when I felt like giving up, your presence in my life enabled me to throw away all the excuses and succeed.

To my family, Steven, Brittney, and Joi, thank you for encouraging me to succeed in all my many ventures.

To my mother, Hazel Ann Smith, I watched you throw away every excuse you could have easily kept; due to the hardships you were dealt with as a young divorced mother, but you succeeded and left a rich legacy for your family.

To all my family members and friends, you all have inspired me to keep moving forward with my dreams and goals.

Photo Gallery of Inspiration

VIPs

MY FAMILY
Steven, Brittney & Joi

My mother Hazel Ann Smith (My Hero)

My Furry Baby Pepsi

Community Service Photos

Delivering Thanksgiving meals to seniors

From the office of the Governor of Virginia

Dr. Pamela recognized by the Governor of Virginia Tim Kaine
for outstanding community service.

Mayor Brenda Perham in Hopewell, VA presents award for
outstanding Community Service

Recognized as outstanding First Lady on the East Coast

Serving in the community of Mombasa, Kenya

Serving with Dr. Marilyn Hickey at crusades in
United Arab Emeritus

No Child Left Alone community event

Baptizing Christians in the Jordan River (Israel)

Serving with young adults in Egypt

"Blessed to Be a Blessing" Drive-Thru campaign for area school in Chester, VA during COVID-19

Personal Achievements

Doctoral Degree (Summa Cum Laude)
with Chancellors Larry and Loretta Ollison

Dr. Pamela being recognized for outstanding customer
service by the Chief Information Officer (Kathy Cutler)
at the Defense Logistics Agency

Dr. Pamela being recognized for outstanding employee at Defense Logistics Agency 43rd Annual Award recognition

Dr. Pamela being recognized for outstanding contributions at the Defense Logistics Agency Energy

Enjoying Life Photos

Grammy Nominee Helen Baylor and Dr. Pamela singing
together during Dr. Pamela's Doctoral Gala

Dr. Pamela and Dr. Helen Baylor

Designer cakes at Dr. Pamela's Gala

Trailblazers Dr. Betty and Apostle Fred Price

Enjoying Wheel of Fortune tryouts

Hollywood Walk of Fame Michael Jackson's Star

My Many Modes of Transportation

Enjoyed my camel ride in Egypt

Enjoyed my ride in a Ferrari

Enjoying our Can-Am Spyder

Enjoyed my first Rolls Royce ride in Beverly Hills

Enjoying Lakewood Church (Joel Osteen) in Houston, Texas

Enjoying New Creation church (Joseph Prince) in Singapore

Enjoying Hill Song Church founder (Bobbie Houston)
Sydney, Australia

Inspire Church, Sydney, Australia

My beloved UCONN games

White House tour with
young teen daughters

Empire State Building
with Joi (daughter)

Enjoying goofy photos with daughters at Ripley's Believe it or
Not in Orlando, Florida

Fun moments with my daughter's (Brittney and Joi)

Pearl Harbor, Hawaii

Enjoying Disney World with hubby

Birthday Queen

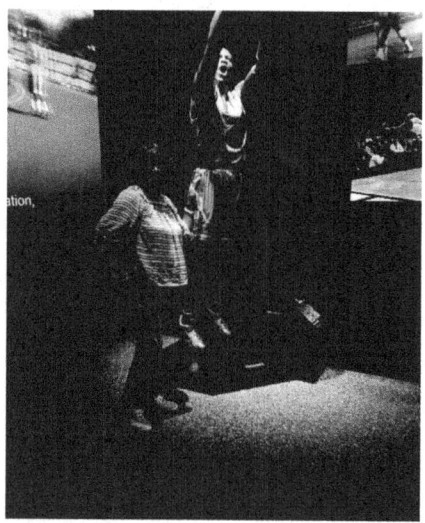

Enjoying MJ at the African American History
Museum in Washington DC

Enjoying Beverly Hills

Enjoying Wahlsburgers restaurant in Los Angeles

Showboat Branson Belle in Branson, Missouri with Minister
Debra Coulter (Aunt)

Trustee Kimberly Tucker (cousin) and Dr. Pamela
enjoying the Grand Canyon

Minister Veronica Legette (1985 friendship began) AKA "sister"
and Dr. Pamela at the famous Faith Dome in Los Angeles

Dr. Pamela enjoying time with long time friends
(1991 friendships began) AKA "sisters" Psalmist Trina Murphy
and Minister Faye Smith

Enjoying Shopping Experiences
All Over The World

Mall of America with Pauletta King (Cousin)

Dr. Pamela enjoying shopping on Rodeo Drive at Jimmy Cho, Chanel and other designer shops in Beverly Hills, CA

Enjoying shopping at the famous Market City in Australia,
Sydney in China Town & Haymarket

Enjoying shopping at the famous Paddy's markets
in Sydney, Australia

Enjoying Shopping in Israel

Enjoying shopping in Singapore…Wow! I had
to purchase another suitcase…

Enjoying shopping in Dubai

Enjoyed shopping at the Gardens by the Bay in Singapore

Enjoying shopping in Egypt

Visiting the famous STAPLES Center

Conquering the famous "Rocky" steps at the Philadelphia
Museum of Art in Philadelphia, PA

Enjoying VOW ladies in Williamsburg, VA

Enjoying VOW ladies on Broadway (The Lion King)

Enjoying VOW ladies in Washington, DC

The Hoover Dam in Nevada

Hollywood Walk of Fame Stars Harry Belafonte

At Prince's estate Paisley in Chanhassen, Minnesota

Chinese Theatre in Hollywood, CA

Enjoyed LE REVE at the Wynn in Las Vegas

The Biltmore Estate in Asheville, NC

Enjoying the King Center and on the steps of the home where
Dr. Martin Luther King Jr. was born on January 15, 1929
(Atlanta, GA)

From left to right Dr. Martin Luther King's sister (Ms. Christine King Farris), Ms. Julia McGill, Dr. Pamela and Minister Debra Coulter at the historic Ebenezer church in Atlanta

Trailblazers…Matthew and Laurie Crouch (President of Trinity Broadcasting Network) at the Garden Tomb in Israel

Famous Louis Lunch in New Haven, CT home of the first hamburger in America with Antoine Scott (my little brother) P.S. Don't ask for ketchup!

Kiki Sheard & Karen Clark (Famous Clark Sisters)

Grand Opening at the Revel at Atlantic City with Psalmist
Kennisha Scott (niece)

Martha Munizzi (Gospel Artist)

Brian Courtney Wilson (Gospel Artist)

Sam Chand (leadership architect)

Chatting with Gospel artist CeCe Winans

Micah Stampley (Gospel Artist)

Dr. Pamela At Her Various
Book Signing Events

Enjoying interacting with the many book supporters…

Countries

Dr. Pamela touches nations around the World

Maria Wiesel (my roommate) enjoying Israel

Welcome to Israel!

Overlooking the Temple Mount in Israel The Sea of Galilee

The Church of the Holy Sepulchre

The Dead Sea

144

A beautiful drama at the Voyager Resort in Mombasa, Kenya

Beautiful mothers in Kenya, Africa

Walking on the shores near the Indian Ocean (Kenya, Africa)

African tribe in Nairobi, Kenya

Enjoying Garden by the Bay in Singapore

AUSTRALIA

The rain forest in Australia with my
Indigenous Australian tour guide

Touring the Great Barrier Reef in Cairns, Australia

Could not resist this photo of the "Grace" van in Sydney, Australia

VOW ladies enjoying Sydney, Australia

In Australia feeding a wallaby

Holding a Koalas (I am not a bear; and my original name is koalas not koala) in Australia

Enjoying a cruise in Sydney, Australia on Sydney Shore

The Schonbrunn Palace in Vienna Austria

Graben's Trinity Column in Vienna, Austria

Vienna, Austria with a live human artist

154

jDr. Pamela at Dr. Miles Munroe (Awesome Mentor)
church in Nassau, Bahamas

Dr. Pamela surprised adopted mother Ms. Julia McGill at age 85
with her first cruise to the Bahamas

Chatting with Dr. Marilyn Hickey in Singapore

Hungary Horse Show contestant in Puszta, Hungary

Enjoying Jamaica

Sydney Australia Opera House

157

Enjoying Trailblazer Dr. Marilyn Hickey in Hungary, Budapest

Welcome to Dubai

مرحبا بكم في دبي

Enjoying Jumeriah Beach in Dubai

Welcome to Egypt

Enjoying the Pyramids Enjoying the Egyptian museum

Enjoying the Nile River cruise

Enjoyed reading about Anwar Sadat the 3rd president of Egypt
at Egyptian Museum in Cairo Egypt

EXCUSES.....
DO NOT MANIFEST RESULTS!

"Dr. Pamela J. Smith-Downing"

~PERSONAL NOTES~

~PERSONAL NOTES~

-PERSONAL NOTES-

Notes

INTRODUCTION

Bible Hub, "Proverbs 13:19," accessed July 20, 2020, https://biblehub.com/proverbs/13-13.htm.

Myles Munroe, "Understanding Your Potential, Discovering the Hidden You", Destiny Image, Revival Press and Treasure House Books, 1998.

CHAPTER 1: WATCH YOUR WORDS

National Center for Voice and Speech, accessed June 28, 2020, http://www.ncvs.org

Bible Hub, "James1:19,"accessed June 28, 2020, http://biblehub.com/commentariesJames/1-19.htm

Pamela Smith-Downing, "Read My Lips No More Debt" (PJD Enterprises LLC, 2020).

CHAPTER 2: PROCASTINATION

Merriam-Webster's Collegiate Dictionary, eleventh edition (Springfield, MA: Merriam- Webster Inc., 2003), s.v. "vision"

CHAPTER 3: THROW AWAY PERSONAL EXCUSES

Kentucky Fried Chicken Story, accessed October 1, 2020, https://en.wikipedia.org/wiki/Colonel_Sanders

CHAPTER 4: THROW AWAY FINANCIAL EXCUSES

Pamela Smith-Downing, "Read My Lips No More Debt" (PJD Enterprises LLC, 2020).

Bible Hub, "Deuteronomy 8:18," accessed October 3, 2020, https://biblehub.com/deuteronomy/8-18.htm.

Pamela Smith-Downing, "Read My Lips No More Debt" (PJD Enterprises LLC, 2020).

CHAPTER 5: THROW AWAY HIGHER LEARNING EXCUSES

Oldest College grad, accessed June 28, 2020, https://www.seattletimes.com/nation-world/95-year-old-now-the-worlds-oldest-college-grad/.

CHAPTER 6: THROW AWAY ENTREPRENUER EXCUSES

Small Business and Entrepreneurship Council, accessed October 3, 2020, https://bit.ly/3iIBe5E

CHAPTER 7: THROW AWAY HEALTH EXCUSES

Obesity in America, accessed November 7, 2020, https://www.cdc.gov/obesity/data/adult.html

Randy Pausch, Jeffrey Zaslow, "The Last Lecture" (Randy Pausch, 2008).

CHAPTER 10: SUCCEED

1. National Coalition of Homeless Veterans, accessed December 18, 2020, http://nchv.org/index.php/news/media/background_and_statistics/#facts

2. Abraham Lincoln, Online.org, accessed December 18, 2020, http://abrahamlincolnonline.org/

3. Bible Hub, "Proverbs 3:4,"accessed June 28, 2020, http://biblehub.com/commentariesJames/1-19.htm

4. Zig Ziglar, accessed June 28, 2020, https://www.goodreads.com/author/show/50316.Zig_Ziglar

Additional Products by
Dr. Pamela J. Smith-Downing

Books

Intimacy with God, a Yearly Journey of
Praying God's Word

Honoring Your Pastor's Wife, The Keys to Her
and Your Success

Gold Nuggets for Leaders and Future Leaders

Ministerial Ethics, a Practical Guide for all Clergy

Read My Lips No More Debt,
Tools to Ending the Debt Cycle

Throw Away the Excuses and Succeed,
Ignite Your Dreams and Goals

Training and Seminar Opportunities

Transformational Coaching Leadership
Training Sessions Financial Coaching

Life Crisis Coaching

To order these products and services
please visit our on-line store

www.pamelajdowning.com

More From
Dr. Pamela J. Smith-Downing

To learn about Dr. Pamela and her ministry visit
pamelajdowning.com and Amazon

Intimacy with God is a journey that will have you falling back in love with God's Word as you read and mediate on your daily devotion throughout the year.

Honoring those in leadership will make room for your gifts. Honoring your Pastor Wives is a resource for all who serve in leadership roles in the local church. Dr. Pamela gives expert advice in this must read for local churches.

The clergy is also called to walk in integrity. Ministerial Ethics reminds the clergy community of the importance of not compromising their calling.

Gold Nuggets for leaders is a must read for leaders in various stages of leadership. Dr. Pamela is a proven leader and gives personal examples of how to lead with passion.

In this timely publication, Dr. Pamela gives tools to have you on a path of becoming totally debt free. Get ready to declare on war on your debt.

About the Author

D
R. PAMELA J. Smith-Downing is a native of New Haven, CT. She is an International speaker, consultant, author, business owner, veteran, crisis and transformational coach to people around the world. She motivates her listeners to reach beyond their circumstances to achieve a more rewarding life. She conducts transformational seminars, financial seminars, mentoring and coaching sessions, workshops and conferences. She carries out her mission to all to live victorious lives in the midst of disappointments and pain.

Dr. Pamela was recognized by several political dignitaries for her leadership and service in her community and abroad. She is a graduate of the USDA Executive Leadership Program and holds an earned Doctorate in Theology from Life Christian University (Summa Cum Laude) and a bachelor's degree in Occupational Technical Studies from Old Dominion University (Cum Laude). Dr. Pamela is also a graduate of Dave Ramsey's Financial Master Coach Training Program.

An entrepreneur with a business mind and an eye for style and excellence, Dr. Pamela is founder and CEO of

PJD Enterprises L.L.C. PJD enterprises is designed to assist customers to go after their dreams and goals with no excuses and lead with passion. She is also founder and CEO of The Jelani and Jade Parent Foundation "AKA" No Child Left Alone. This foundation mission is to provide superior service and support to children and parents; to alleviate the on-going tragedies of children being left alone.

Dr. Pamela also conducts the Ministry of Excellence conferences, which are designed to train up business owners, church leaders and those seeking to go to another level in every area of their lives. Dr. Pamela is the founder of Victorious Over-comers in the Word (VOW) Women's conference. The VOW conference is designed to help women stop breaking vows and become a VOW.

Dr. Pamela has written six books and counting, including her signature book "Gold Nuggets for Leaders and Future Leaders". She has authored books on leadership, and church protocol. She also built a vast library of materials designed to prepare men and women to live victorious in the areas of leadership, finance and excellence. Her training materials are widely used in corporate settings and churches.

Dr. Pamela shares her life and love with her husband Steven, and her two daughters Brittney and Joi. She enjoys spending quality time with family and friends, travelling internationally, reading, and event planning. Dr. Pamela's life vision is to help others throw away the excuses and succeed!

Made in the USA
Monee, IL
13 February 2021